A Read-Together Book for Parents & Children

Sometimes a Family Has to Split Up

by Jane Werner Watson

Robert E. Switzer, M.D.
Former Director of the Children's Division
The Menninger Clinic

J. Cotter Hirschberg, M.D.
William C. Menninger Distinguished Professor
of Psychiatry, The Menninger Clinic

with pictures by Cat Bowman Smith

Crown Publishers, Inc., New York

A Read-Together Book for Parents & Children™
Created in cooperation with The Menninger Foundation

The Dorothy Wright Treatment and Endowment Fund defrays a part of the care
and treatment cost at the Children's Division
of The Menninger Clinic, Box 829, Topeka, Kansas 66601.
Part of the income of the sale of this book goes to that fund.

Published by Crown Publishers, Inc., 225 Park Avenue South, New York, New York
10003 and represented in Canada by the Canadian MANDA Group
CROWN, A READ-TOGETHER BOOK FOR PARENTS & CHILDREN, and logo are trade-
marks of Crown Publishers, Inc.

Manufactured in Hong Kong

Library of Congress Cataloging-in-Publication Data
Watson, Jane Werner, 1915–
    Sometimes a family has to split up/by Jane Werner Watson, Robert E. Switzer, J.
Cotter Hirschberg; with pictures by Cat Bowman Smith.—1st ed.
    p. cm.—(A Read-together book for parents and children)
    Summary: A young boy describes his feelings of fear, guilt, and confusion when he
discovers that his parents are getting a divorce.
    1. Divorce—Juvenile literature. 2. Separation (Psychology)—Juvenile literature.
3. Children of divorced parents—Attitudes—Juvenile literature. [1. Divorce.] I. Switzer,
Robert E., 1918–   . II. Hirschberg, J. Cotter, 1915–   . III. Smith, Cat Bowman, ill.
IV. Title. V. Series: Read-together book for parents & children.
HQ814.W35 1988
306.8′9—dc19
ISBN 0-517-56811-X
10 9 8 7 6 5 4 3 2 1
First Edition

NOTE TO PARENTS

Youngsters used to grow up believing that marriages were made in heaven, that romantic love struck like a lightning bolt from the blue, and that once love had led to marriage, that partnership lasted until "death do us part."

Today children grow up in a world in which the dissolution of marriage is almost as much the rule as the exception. More important to the children, the end of a marriage that has produced offspring means the breakup of a family. There are not many American preschoolers today who do not have some acquaintance with a split or one-parent family. To a child in a family that is breaking up, this crumbling of the base of his or her secure, private world is bound to be wounding. Even to small friends, it is confusing and distressing.

Frequently parents, caught in a situation for which they can see no other solution than escape, forget at least temporarily the hypersensitivity of the child. They forget how terrifying it can be to be in the midst of an unhappy situation one does not understand but which nonetheless involves one directly. In the concentration on their own hurt, parents may overlook the searing pain for a child of being torn between conflicting loyalties to two antagonistic parents, and the possibility that the child may feel responsible and be overwhelmed by secret guilt feelings.

Anxious to justify their own actions, each parent may attempt to destroy the child's love for the other parent. And though they may long for a way to explain the situation temperately and fairly to the child, this may be beyond them while they are themselves in the tangled center of the turmoil.

This little book—in the form of a very simple, non-judgmental story—attempts to provide a framework for the much-needed calm discussion of the situation. Similarities to the child's own problems, or differences from them, will provide opportunities for conversation. If separation or divorce is imminent in a child's circle—or in his or her own family—the story can be introduced casually, read through, and used as a springboard for questions, answers, and growing understanding.

Perhaps the child will request rereadings, as a means of opening up further opportunities for warm, objective, and supportive discussions of the problems, the inevitable pain, and the prospects for a brighter future.

Many children entertain fantasies of the family reunited long after this has become a practical impossibility, and it is desirable to bring these into the open and deal with them sympathetically but sensibly, to speed a sound and relatively happy adjustment.

ROBERT E. SWITZER, M.D.
Former Director of the Children's Division
The Menninger Clinic

J. COTTER HIRSCHBERG, M.D.
William C. Menninger Distinguished Professor of Psychiatry
The Menninger Clinic

I used to live with my mother
and my daddy.
We had a lot of good times.

Of course sometimes
someone in the family
didn't feel good or got cross.
I guess that happens in all families.
I didn't like those times.
I didn't even like it
when I was the cross one.

But usually we talked things over
and we all felt better.
Things have changed now.
For a while I thought
the bad things happened
because I started
to go to preschool.

I hadn't wanted to go at first.
My mother said I'd like it.
I wasn't sure.
But I said I'd try.

Well, I did like it.
There were lots of toys.
I liked the teacher.
I learned a lot.
And I made new friends.
I found out that not all the children
live with their mothers and dads
together.

Susan's mother picks her up
after preschool every day.
Susan's mother is very young.
She is still in school.
Susan doesn't have a dad at home.

Jeff's mother usually picks him up.
But on Fridays his dad comes for him.
Jeff spends weekends with his dad.
He has a stepdad
at home with his mother.
I didn't think I'd like that.

I was always glad to get
home from school.
My mom and dad both work,
but a nice lady named Miss Mary
was always waiting for me.

Then when my mom and dad
came home from work
we'd eat together
and be together until my bedtime.

After a while, though,
my mother and dad
weren't always home for dinner.
Mostly it was my dad
who wasn't there.
Mom said he was working late,
but I could see that
she didn't like it.

By the time he did come,
she'd be cross.
After I went to bed
those nights, I could hear
them quarreling.
They both shouted a lot.
I was supposed to be asleep,
but it made me hurt inside.

I couldn't hear what they said,
but they sounded angry,
and I heard doors banging.
I always went to sleep
after a while,
but I woke up with a heavy lump
inside me.

I didn't want to go to school
those days.
I was afraid my home
wouldn't be there
when I came home.
I told my dad that.
He hugged me tight.

But he didn't look at me.
From then on my mom and dad
quarreled a lot.
Or else they were silent and sad.
They didn't feel like playing.
I decided they didn't love me
anymore.

That made the lump inside me
come back worse than ever.
I felt bad even at school.
Sometimes I shouted at my friends.
Or I took toys from them.
It made me cross
to see them happy
when I was hurting inside.

I didn't even want to go home
those days.
My mother was sad and cross.
Sometimes she didn't speak
to me or my dad.
That was even worse
than a quarrel.
Now I knew she didn't love me.

My dad was sad too.
He didn't want to play ball
after school.
I thought it must be my fault.
My stomach ached almost every day.

Then one night
there was a worse quarrel.
The next morning at breakfast
my mother and dad told me
they were going to get a divorce.
They said they just weren't
happy together anymore.

I thought it was my fault.
I couldn't say anything.
"It's not your fault, Chip,"
my mother said.
"It's not anybody's fault,"
my dad said.
"But if we have different homes
we won't quarrel anymore."

"We'll still be friends,"
my mother said.
"We'll still both love you,"
my dad told me.

"But we won't have a home.
Where will I live?" I asked them very quietly.
"We've talked that over,"
Mother said.
"You and I will stay here."
"I'm moving to an apartment,"
Dad said.

"Oh," I said.
I couldn't say anything else.
The bad feeling was back.
I wanted us all
to go on living together,
but without the quarreling.

Well, all that happened
a while ago.
I know now that things
just can't be
like they used to be.

It still makes me sad sometimes,
but it doesn't make me hurt inside
like the quarreling did.
My mom and I live together now.

Miss Mary comes every day
to pick me up at school.
I help her around the house
until my mom comes home.

My dad lives in an apartment in town.

I visit him.

I have a place there

for some of my toys.

It isn't like home,

but my dad and I have fun.

It's not as good

as when we were all living happily together.

But it's better than it was.

And I know now that
what happened was not my fault.
Sometimes a family
just has to split up.